MY WALK

OF

FAITH

Valerie Ashworth More

My Walk of faith

Valerie Ashworth More

This book was first published in Great Britain in paperback during May 2022.

The moral right of Valerie Ashworth More is to be identified as the author of this work and has been asserted by her in accordance with the Copyright, Designs and Patents Act of 1988.

ISBN: 979-8831853278

CONTENTS

MY WALK OF FAITH

*I Can't Go Any Further Andrew, You
Carry on Without Me. No, He Says,
You've Come This Far, You Can Do It,*

And I Did!!!

ACKNOWLEDGEMENTS

Thank you to my Fantastic Family and Friends who have gone through so much with me over the years.

My Two Sons Roy & Scott, Daughter in Law Deanna & my 3 Precious Grandchildren Jack, Elouisa & Thorfinn.

My Three Sisters Ella, Margaret, Brenda and her husband Wallace.

My Niece Tara and Nephew Kieran.

John and Barbara Ashworth who without his Encouragement this book would never have been Published.

My Treasured friends Ann and Stuart.

My Church Family who never fail to amaze me in their Faithfulness.

To Babs Stevenson my Mentor.

Stuart and Helen from RTF who showed me how to live again.

And to Andrew my Husband who I dedicate this book to, you are truly Amazing, thank you for being there always and without you I know I wouldn't be alive today.

God Bless

I love you all so much.

FOREWORD

It's a bonny summer's day here in the beautiful North of Scotland in the totally unique Orkney Islands, separated from the Scottish Mainland by the waters of the Pentland Firth, which to many an experienced seafarer is one of the scariest waters they will sail on. I feel so blessed sitting out in my back garden in the beautiful North End of Shapinsay overlooking Veantro Bay where we are blessed to call home. It feels so peaceful and tranquil, the South-Easterly breeze blowing softly against my skin, the sun beating down illuminating on the soft still water of the Bay, yet it can change so dramatically in a matter of hours as the wind gets up suddenly and starts howling. The Bay is suddenly full of wild white horses lashing against the rocks.

In the distance, fields of contrasting colours of green glisten like emeralds in the sun. The golden wheat, which has not yet been harvested, ripples in the breeze. Some fields have already been cut down for this year's silage while others are left to grow.

In the neighbouring fields there's black cows basking in the sunshine, happy to be outside after being inside all winter. Looking up at the unblemished sky, so clear except for a few clouds looking like great balls of fluffy cotton wool, not moving. Everything is so still and peaceful just the way I like my life now.

The birds chirping happily away in the trees; Smog and Millie our two cats sleeping lazily in the sun soaking it all up; our goats Daisy and Annie in the field munching away on the juicy grass. The hens wandering about looking for bugs enjoying this glorious July day.

And sitting beside me our faithful Border Collie Ben, panting in the heat, looking for a bit of shade under my seat but always hoping I will get up and throw the ball for him to chase.

Away in the distance Wideford Hill on Orkney Mainland and beyond that the hills of Hoy, the island where I grew up. I feel like I have come full circle, my young life on one island and now ending up on another.

Orkney really is a uniquely different way of life, a group of Islands surrounded by sea, where if you keep going north you will get to the Shetland Islands and beyond that Iceland. There is so much history on these islands from the Churchill Barriers from World War two to a way further back thousands of years- Skara Brae, Ring of Brodgar and Maeshowe to name a few places.

The winters in Orkney can be harsh with cutting blustery winds and driving rain thrashing against you when you go outside, but at the same time beautiful and in the summer out of this world sunsets and glorious days of sunshine beating down on you, we are truly blessed to live in the uniqueness of this place.

It feels so magical, life so quiet and slow paced giving you time to gather your thoughts and reflect but also so much to do if you want to get involved with Island events. There's always something going on all year round, with local dances and ceilidh's, fetes, Orkney's farmers' market, our yearly shows, fundraising events, not to mention the local bands and musicians. There is a lot of talent amongst these islands, a real sense of community spirit and we are very self-sufficient. As well as our own hospital, two main secondary schools, supermarkets, a cinema, and a swimming pool, we have an airport, and a local ferry service going to the Scottish Mainland and around Orkney sailing to the Outer and Inner isles.

At 53 I have come a long way from that little girl who used to play on the beach with my sisters in Brimms on Hoy where I spent my childhood. So much has happened that sometimes I can't believe it's me. When you're young you have so many expectations and dreams about life, you quite rightly are so innocent and full of hope for all the things you want to achieve as you get older. I always wanted to be a nurse from as far back as I remember but alas it wasn't meant to be. But now as I'm older I wished I had pursued my dream. That's why no matter what never give up on your dreams, anything is possible if you want it enough. Life is so precious and it's only now I can appreciate how true that is.

This is about the journey I have been on for the last 40 years. It's not a self-help book, more about showing you that life after an addiction is possible, that even in the darkest times of your life, there is Hope, you can turn your life around for the better and be happy in yourself, and I am living proof of that.

When You Feel Your "Drowning" In Life's
Situations, Don't Worry Your Saviour is there to
Save You, I Am Saved by his Amazing Grace.

CHAPTER ONE

My Pretend Mask

For years I was a lost soul trying to get on with my life, wearing a mask being happy Val, but inside feeling dead and empty. The only time I felt really fulfilled was when I had my two precious sons, such unconditional love, but in the end only one person could rescue me, "JESUS," I was broken inside and didn't understand how anybody could love me, then my Saviour came along and took away my heavy burden of Guilt and Shame.

I first started drinking when I was in my teens, but it was never a problem (or so I thought), it filled a void inside me. Everyone else my age was doing it, going to the local dances on the island having fun, it was my way of trying to fit in, even back then I always felt a bit different, so I thought that being part of the in crowd surely then I would get accepted by everyone. Looking back that's always been my problem a feeling of wanting to belong and to fit into the mould of what others thought of me, that's why putting on that mask helped, I could be somebody else for a while, be who everyone else wanted me to be. That's why I suppose drinking became such a big part of my life even at such a young age, it broke down the barriers that I had up, for even though on the outside I was to my friends this great party girl always out for a laugh and out for a good time, inside I was crying out someone help me please. I felt so lonely and empty, never felt that I belonged to anyone or anything,

I got my first job when I was fourteen and I look back on that time with great fondness. It was in the local Parton factory in Brimms, not the most glamorous of jobs, bit smelly (I can't stand the smell of Partons boiling to this day). It was a Saturday job, and I can still remember the laughs we had. It was certainly a good lesson in growing up quickly, and one of the only times, that I really felt a real sense of belonging. I really felt a real sense of family working there, what a laugh I had when I went in on a Saturday morning because there usually had been a dance and then a party after it the night before and the stories that were going round were so funny. I used to save my money up to go across to the mainland for the event of the year "The

County Show."

People used to come up on holiday especially for it. Me and my friends would go in and feel so grown up, going round all the stalls, and looking at the animals, but what was on our minds was getting into the beer tent and having a few cans of lager. We never thought it was wrong, not being aged to drink, and looking back, even then I was looking for that escape from being me. Afterwards it was going to the dance in the evening and dancing all night, usually with boys you didn't know, but nothing ever really happened - maybe a quick kiss, but back then I was more interested in having a good time rather than being with boys. It brings back good memories; it was so busy; it was so good to get lost in the crowd with nobody knowing who you were. When I met anybody new and they asked what my name was, I never gave them my real name, not until I got to know them better. I was far better at being someone else wearing that mask than I could ever be being who I really was. I wanted to be the opposite of me. I had fair straight hair, so I wanted to have black curly hair. I hated my freckles, my figure, always thought my sister was so pretty and skinny while I was big boned like my dad or, so I was told often enough. I just wanted to hide behind a make belief person because then no one would know the real me.

My dad died when I was twelve which looking back was when all my insecurities began. When you lose someone at such an early age, such as a parent, it is going to make a significant impact in your life. You're just starting to find out about yourself, starting puberty which can be very scary, all these hormones and emotions going through your body. Me and my mum were never that close which is nobody's fault, just life. I know deep inside that she did love us, but in a lot of ways I reminded her of my dad so it must have been hard for her when he died, dealing with all that and having a daughter that was a constant reminder of him. Apart from my older sister I didn't have anyone to speak to, which I did sometimes but she had her own life to be getting on with so just pretended that everything was fine. I was a big brave girl, the kind of person that other folk could go to with their problems, which I loved because for a while I could forget all my worries and self-doubt. Nowadays you can get counselling if you want it if you have a family bereavement, but back in the eighties it was all so different. You just got on with it hoping that eventually things would work out and things would get better with time. But I really believe that losing my dad at an early age shaped me for what I was to become at least into my forties, someone who relied on and needed alcohol to give me confidence and a feeling of security. To hide that sense of emptiness that was inside me. A void inside me that has only gone now after all these years, that for me no human being could fill. As much as I love them, especially my children more than life itself, only God could fill that void, a peace inside me and that feeling that I am worth it.

When we lived in Brimms I felt happy and loved. I worshipped my older sister; it was just the two of us then before my two peedie sisters were born. We used to play on the beach, building sandcastles and paddling in the sea. There used to always be a few of us kids there playing, lovely innocent times which I still look back on and cherish to this day, happy memories, my sister would tell a different story having this annoying little sister following her around everywhere.

I can remember when I was about eight my dad taking me out on his little dinghy to go fishing, what great fun it was until we got too close to the skerries. It felt a bit scary not knowing what was going to happen next, but he kept rowing away from the skerry (no mean feat I'm sure looking back). Eventually he rowed us to safety. I felt so proud of him as he got us back to the shore. It's funny the things you remember as a child, but I am so glad I have that memory of him, a nice feeling of being protected, how that was going to change very soon, and a different life was beckoning. Life as we knew it was going to change dramatically.

When we moved from Brimms down to the local housing scheme that's when things changed for me and my sisters. My mums drinking started with a vengeance, a pretty horrendous time of parties in our house and folk getting drunk not just at weekends but through the week as well when we had to get up for school in the morning. There was always something to celebrate, someone's birthday, a wedding or just a good old get together, any excuse really. At first it seemed like good fun but after a while it started to be a dread. It was really hard on us all, I used to cry myself to sleep just wanting it all to go away, even at times wishing I was dead - a horrible feeling in the pit of my stomach, the music getting louder and louder usually Scottish music ,them all singing away having a great time, us in bed trying to sleep but long forgotten about by them. In the morning having to get up for school feeling so tired, dreading coming home from school already in case it was going to happen all over again. How I used to envy my friends going home to a nice warm "drink free" house with their tea on the table. Getting off the school bus and walking up to my house was awful because I had that dread in the pit of my stomach not knowing if there was going to be anyone home or not. To this day I can't stand a locked door, it still fills me with a cold fear and brings me back to that little girl standing knocking at my door just wanting to get in and feel safe and secure. In the warmth of my cosy house, the relief when it was open was immense, how sad it is that when all you want when your peedie is to get into the safety of your own home, to just be warm and feel safe and secure and have a full belly. It's not much to ask when you're that age, but that's where all my self-doubt and insecurities about myself came from, that lost little girl just wanting a bit of love and security from her mum. As I am older now I can see that she had her own problems and used drink to block the things out that she had to deal with.

I used to take our darling dog Lady a golden Labrador for a walk enjoying the Solitude, knowing deep down there was an emptiness inside me, singing nobody's Child out loud, if anyone had seen me they would have thought I was bonkers, or maybe they thought that about me anyway, I still don't know to this day how I knew the words to that song.

I loved our dog so much, her name suited her, she was a Lady, what unconditional love she gave us as a family, when I was younger I didn't appreciate the power of love an animal can give you, they don't judge , all they ask is to be loved back, which I would find out when I got older and had my own dogs, we also had a black cat called Mittens, he was a Character and was such a comfort to my two younger sisters,

There was always home brew being made in our house, I suppose it was cheaper back then than buying it as we didn't have much money and making it yourself was a better option. I remember when I was about nine scooping some out of the barrel with a jug (the way my mum used to do it before it was even bottled). I gulped it down. I think from what I recall that was the first time I felt tipsy. I went to the shop with my mum, and I fell against the counter and the local minister said to me are you Fu? (Meaning have you been drinking), I just laughed feeling happy inside thinking this is a nice feeling. And here I suppose lies the problem, that euphoria and thinking this drinking is not so bad at all, I feel happy inside.

But it didn't take long for me to start hating drink and everything that came with it, how it changed people, but there were spells that we were really happy when there was no drinking. I loved those times, felt secure again, let my guard down thinking that everything was going to be okay, coming home from school to a nice smell of homemade soup, the fire on, sitting at the table me my mum and sisters having our tea and having a normal family time. This could go on for a couple of weeks but alas the drinking always started again. I resented people coming to our house partying, thinking they were the bees knees, giving us some pennies to go to the local shop to get rid of us for a while, making them feel better by giving us a treat when inside I was screaming for them to get out of my house so me and my sisters could just feel normal and watch a bit of telly after school and get to bed on time. Blaming myself for my mum drinking, always feeling it was somehow my fault. All these bad things had to be my fault. I never really felt loved by her then, just wasn't wanted. Why oh why was I ever born?

 I felt I had no self-worth and didn't feel I had any value, I started going into myself, felt a real sense of rejection from my mum and also my dad for dying, he couldn't have loved me if he had left us. When you're young, you just see black and white. He wouldn't have died if he had wanted to be my dad, so all these things I was feeling inside must be true if my dad had gone and my mum didn't really have time for me. Little did I know back then that she was hurting inside as well, communication is a wonderful thing. I just wish we had talked more as a family and opened up to each other and then maybe I wouldn't have gone through life until the age I am now to realise I do have value and self-worth.

I have forgiven everyone for it all now, especially my mum who I blamed all through my years growing up and as part of my adult life. She passed away three years ago and I forgave her before she died, she said she was sorry and that's all I needed to hear. I know now it wasn't anyone's fault, just circumstances. Orkney has a big drinking culture, but I suppose it's i communities wherever you live, you just think it's happening to you. Back then in the seventies and eighties there was no social media or mobile phones so the world felt like a very lonely place I just felt glad to have a television to watch, but   life can be cruel. Now I know without forgiveness it just eats you up inside like a horrible poison until you feel all bitter and blame everyone else for the way your life turns out when at the end of the day only you can choose the path you want to follow, with God's help of course. For even though we went to Church and Sunday school I never thought he existed, how could he if I were going through all this sadness and emptiness. But for God to come into your life you must first reach out to him and ask him for help.

How strange is it though that the very thing I hated most in life was drink, but I turned to that myself in later years? How ironic that the think I loathed was going to be what I turned to doing myself, something that I was going to rely on so much to make me feel better about myself. Life has a habit of doing that to you. I just wish I had known what a dark road it was going to take me on.

When you live on an island you attend the local primary school which I really enjoyed. I met my best friend Ann there when I was four and we're still friends to this day. I used to go and play with her at her house and loved going there, her parents were so lovely to me, and I used to think this is the way I want to be when I grow up. Such a loving couple. We were so different, but she got me, knew what I went through at home but never judged me, just treated me as her best friend. I felt normal around her, not having to be something I wasn't. Looking back, I'm so grateful I had her at primary school, my ally in life, but back then when you turned twelve you had to go across to the mainland of Orkney to "the big school" in Kirkwall. I loved it.

We stayed in the hostel through the week Monday to Friday. To me, it was a lifeline getting away from home where few people knew me. It was like starting afresh, I got peace, not having to worry about locked doors or when I was going to get my tea or what time I was going to get to bed. It was freedom. Sounds strange, looking back, saying that I wasn't a great fan of the Secondary School, but it was bearable. A lot of the kids didn't really like the hostel, they missed being home, but to me for those four years, it was my home. I did miss my little sisters though, and my mum at times, because when she was sober, she was a good mum.

I so desperately wanted to be a nurse, I would go out on work placements to the local hospital and absolutely loved it. I always looked at the nurses in awe. To me they were my idols, just like superheroes and I felt so grown up going to the canteen with them at break time. I couldn't wait to leave school and start my training and to wear a uniform like them. That was my dream, and I was so sure I was going to do that, little did I know back then that I would be spending time with nurses in the hospital, not in the work capacity but as a patient with them caring for me. The shame I used to feel laying in that hospital bed when all I wanted to do was help other folk to get better and here was I an absolute wreck having to be cared for my dreams shattered.

Secondary school days were a happy time in my life. I

made new friends, me and Ann shared a room in the hostel, still friends but spreading our wings a little bit as well - meeting new folk. I met another lifelong friend when I was at the Secondary School. She was from a district in Orkney called Orphir and we hit it off right away and were like sisters at school. I used to go and stay with her at weekends which I loved. Her family were so good to me and made me feel so at home, I have never forgotten them and still see them sometimes in the town.

Going home at the weekends was okay as well. I was growing up and had started going out to the local youth club on a Saturday night. It was fun playing badminton, getting "Tuck shop" our sweeties and juice. It was wholesome fun hanging out at the local YM, then when I was about fourteen, we started to go to the local dances then parties, drinking a couple of cans of lager on a night. To me that felt so grown up, running around in the older boys' cars, listening to Fleetwood Mac, Queen, ZZ Top. It really felt this was living on the edge. How naive I was, but back then I thought I could take on the world. I was starting to realise I could have fun with alcohol. One thing I never did was take up smoking, well I tried it once. Me and my friend were walking home from the Youth Club, it was a twenty-minute walk from there to our houses and she had a packet of cigarettes. She was smoking a bit but not the whole time and for some reason - it seems a bit mad now looking back - we decided we had to smoke the whole packet.

Crazy behaviour, but at that age when you're a teenager you do some bizarre stuff. So, we smoked ten each in half an hour. Well, I was dizzy as soon as I got home and sick and the smell of the nicotine on my hands and clothes was disgusting, so that was my one and only time I ever tried smoking. Never again. I think it was a real blessing. I am so thankful I never took up smoking, especially since it was seen as such a cool thing to do back then. I think even at that age I didn't fit into the "norm." I must admit I did enjoy being just that little bit different, pretending to enjoy it but feeling like an outsider. When I was older someone said to me how weird it is that you don't smoke since you're an alcoholic the two usually go together. I thought at the time 'thank God for that'. I'm not your usual stereotype. Another think I never dabbled in was drugs, never really mind it being available or anyone having any, thank goodness. I dread to think what would have happened if I had tried that, especially now that I realise, I have an addictive personality. It could all have been a lot worse, since all I ever wanted was to fit in, be part of the gang.

Life continued like that for a couple of years, still my dreaming of becoming a nurse, and going back and forth to the big school on the mainland. I would say this was an enjoyable time in my life. I felt I was in control; my mum still drank but I was older and could handle it better. It was my peedie sisters that were having a harder time at home. I even went on a school trip to London. I have a stepbrother, John, who lives there so he took me and Ann on a sightseeing tour that was good fun.

I can't ever mind getting really drunk, more merry when I was a teenager, but I did enjoy the feeling of confidence drink gave me. People liked this confident Val, but it was just a façade, not the real me, just a lonely girl who was about to become a woman and what a Baptism of Fire that was about to be.

When I was sixteen, I found out I was pregnant. I knew deep down I was but tried to hide it. If I didn't speak about it, then it couldn't be happening. Talk about burying your head in the sand. I was going out with a local older boy, and I didn't even tell him at the start. I just felt really scared, the thought of bringing another human life into this world terrified me. I hadn't even figured out what life was about yet; all these thoughts were going through my head. Even though it was over thirty years ago, I can still remember all of it like it was yesterday. Imagine this scared sixteen-year-old, feeling like I had no one to turn to. I couldn't even bring myself to tell my big sister, which seems so silly now as I know she would have been supportive of me. I just couldn't bring myself to say these words "I think I am pregnant," but as nature was taking its course I started to show, and my auntie started suspecting and persuaded me to go to the doctor. I went with her and I'm so glad I did. He was so lovely to me; he gave me a few options and one was an abortion. This was the point I really fell in love with my unborn baby, I knew there was no way I was going to terminate the pregnancy. From that moment on I was this protective mum to be who would do anything for her baby, even being so young. Of course, my dreams of becoming a nurse came to an end as well or so I thought. I wish someone had told me that I could be a mum and have a career as well. It wouldn't be easy, but it could have been done. Being pregnant and then getting married (something I didn't want to do deep inside, but it was expected of us from our families) at a young age, before it was even legal for me to drink, put a stop to partying with my friends. If I'm honest it was a bit of a culture shock. I hadn't even started out on my own life but here I was married with a baby on the way. It took a long while for it to sink in, but as usual I had my happy Val mask on, so no one noticed that I was terrified and feeling so alone. It's really strange how you can feel so alone when there's always folk around you, pretending that everything is fine. Looking back, I know I didn't love my husband and he certainly didn't love me or our married life. I think he felt trapped. Of course, me and my mum weren't that close, so I never really spoke to her about how I was feeling. I think she thought I had made my bed so I had to lie in it, which to a certain extent that was true, but a little support would have been so good.

A lot of the older islander residents on Hoy were so kind to me and took me under their wing and for that I am so grateful. That's the blessing of living on a small island, everyone knows you and your business, but in this case I was glad. I suppose a lot of them were worried how this young sixteen-year-old was going to manage. They weren't the only ones, my sisters were delighted and excited at the thought of this little baby joining the family, which after what they had been through losing our dad was a nice feeling for them to be getting a baby into the family. It was someone to give all their love too, which they did. I eventually had a little boy and the love I felt for him was something I had never experienced before, that emptiness I had been feeling inside was gone. My perfect little baby boy. It was a shock and a relief to me to have those feelings towards him because being so young I wasn't sure how I would feel but the pure joy of having him overshadowed all the doubts I had when I was pregnant. Not that I didn't want him, just at that age you're still a child yourself. All those doubts melted away as soon as I saw my darling little boy, I was a mum, and it didn't take long for me to know that I would do anything to protect my child I loved him more than life itself.

Apart from my son I was so unhappy being married. By now I knew my husband at the time wasn't ready for settling down, didn't really bond with the baby. His family did and was very supportive, but it just wasn't enough, and I left with my son and moved back in with my mum. I didn't really drink at this point. I was happy being a new mum and spending time with my baby. My sisters were so supportive to me and without them I really don't know what I would have done, and then a few years later I had another son from a different relationship, and I felt happy and fulfilled. I had the same feelings for my second baby as my first, pure unconditional love. I loved being a mum something which did surprise me as it wasn't something I had ever really thought about when I was little. I can remember someone saying to me when the boys were peedie how

do you feel about being a mum, do you find it hard?
My first reaction was no they're a gift from God (that
was before I even had God in my life). It's the one
thing in life I did right becoming a mum. My happiest
times were when the boys were peedie - our own little
unit.

But I always had that nagging doubt inside that I was
inadequate, not good enough, so the mask would come
out again. I would pretend to be happy Val. Life was
good for a while, the first few years of the boy's life I
didn't really drink, just socially out to our local pub,
dances, family get togethers. I was in a happy
relationship; I loved the home we had together. We had
a few lovely holidays, our favourite had to be when
we went to Stirling Castle and the Wallace Monument,
the film "Braveheart" had just been released, the story
of the Scottish Rebel William Wallace ,it was amazing
steeped in history, walking up the steps to the
Monument the boys were so excited, what an awesome
country we live in, so many places to go and explore, or
if we didn't get away South, we went up to Rackwick, a
really magical part of the Island of Hoy, totally different
to anywhere else in Orkney, going for a paddle in the
burn or a dip in the sea ,which usually was quite warm,
collecting pebbles and having a picnic, The Winter
evenings were spent playing board games beside the

cosy fire, Monopoly being the favourite, or the local
drama group called HAWEG short for Hoy and Walls
Entertainment Group, an absolutely amazing time and
we has so much fun, the boys and I took part in the
local Pantomimes, this must have been one of the best
times of my life, I loved performing on stage,
becoming someone else for a while, most of the
children on the Island took part as well as a lot of the
adults, there was a real sense of Community Spirit,
what fabulous times, thank you to everyone who made
me feel like I belonged and made me forget for a short
while, it was all about having fun and making
memories, making the boys feeling secure, which is
what a child needs and love, that's what turns them
into well-grounded adults, special times, there is no
better feeling than seeing pure joy and enjoyment in
your child's eyes, these were the memories that kept me
going through some very dark times,

We had a nice circle of friends, went out drinking
sociably but never drinking to excess, just the usual
island parties sometimes at our house. It was always
good fun, but I suppose looking back I was enjoying
drinking just a little bit too much. I had a wonderful
next-door neighbour who to this day I love dearly. She

had two children as well, so we were always popping into each other's houses. She was and has always been such a supportive friend and I am so glad we were there for each other. So, life was okay, the usual ups and downs, and if I'm honest I was starting to drink too much. At this point, I would take any excuse to have a drink, but I was still managing to work and bring up the boys because I was still only drinking at the weekends. As they went into their teens I started drinking more regularly, but the boys were happy. I always had that nagging feeling that there was something just not right, but carried on as normal, drinking a bit more that I should be, always thinking it was okay as long as I did it sociably or with someone else.

When my relationship broke down the drinking really started. I suppose it was a good excuse to drink, at weekends and wine - thinking that's not strong drink. I was so unhappy inside. That big void was back. I really think I was having some kind of breakdown, all these emotions that I had bottled up inside from when I was little after my dad died, were slowly coming to the surface. I absolutely hated myself, the boys were upset at the way things had turned out and I felt terribly guilty about that.

Around this time, I started seeing my first husband again, and I think he would agree it was through drink fuelled eyes, not love anyway, he moved into our home. Things went downhill then. It was a hard adjustment for the boys to have someone else move into the family home for it had just been me and them for a wee while. In hindsight it should have never happened, and I wish I could turn the clock back on that time for my boys' sake. We got married again, I felt numb inside just going through the emotions, but the drinking was getting worse and worse. The transition from wine to vodka didn't take long as I was starting to need a bigger hit from the drink. Here was I, someone who hated this stuff, starting to rely on it more and more. A bottle of wine at the weekend first, but that soon became a bottle every night which escalated to the point I couldn't even get out of bed in the morning without needing a drink. I put on my mask when I was out, hoping nobody noticed I had been drinking. It was spiralling out of control, a vicious circle that I just couldn't break. It was awful, I was also using the drink as a pain relief from the pain of my marriage, hiding behind the door of drink and alcohol abuse. By this time knowing I had made such a big mistake getting married again, crying, and drinking more, seeing no way out. I used to go to the local shop to buy the drink making all these excuses as to why I was buying it. But of course, they knew fine I was buying it for myself. So, the Guilt and Shame I felt just got worse and the only thing that would stop these feelings was to have another drink. Alcohol became my best friend something I could turn to that made me feel better.

My close family and friends were getting concerned about me and my drinking, but I always brushed them off convincing them everything was fine. But of course, thinks were far from all right. I so wish now I had spoken to someone, but it's hard to admit your marriage is a sham, scared of someone coming through that front door drunk not knowing what frame of mind they are in. Always know it is never your fault, no one deserves to be frightened in their own home, but at the time I felt it was all I deserved, a low life drunk that's what I was, or at least that's what I was told often enough.

Looking back now I know that this was the enemy at work making me feel like this. Drink makes you do things that you would never normally do. I didn't realise at the time that my best friend was going to turn into my worst enemy, a nightmare that I wouldn't wish on anybody. A big black gaping hole swallowing you up, that you have no control over and before you know it you are falling into the pits of hell, scrambling as you try to get out. When drink gets a grip of you it's something that you don't expect. You think you should cut down but by that time it's too late, your body craves for drink, you go to sleep with such good intentions but wake up with your whole body shaking, sweating from head to toe. The tremors start, so you hope against hope that you have a drink in the house, if not at hand hidden somewhere. I managed to stop for a while but never for too long. The enemy's grip was getting stronger and stronger and the Val I knew was slipping away. I was losing my identity.

The things you do under the influence of drink makes me cringe now. Even going into the town and going on the boat was like doing a marathon sometimes. I couldn't even do that without needing to take a drink with me in my bag, usually vodka and a little bit of coke disguised in a Pepsi bottle, thinking nobody knew but of course I must have been stinking of alcohol. On this one day on my way back from the town after buying a bottle of vodka and filling up my "coke" bottle, trying to hide the fact that I was drunk, I was getting off the ferry, climbing the stairs and I took a tumble and fell straight down to the bottom. I was so drunk I didn't even care. I had no self-respect. A very kind crew member (if he ever reads this thank you) helped me up and took me home where thankfully no one was there so I went to bed to sleep it off. When I woke up and I remembered what had happened. I felt so ashamed. How low could I go? How could I ever face going on that ferry ever again? But of course, I did after having a few drinks to give me the courage, after that I could do anything or so I thought.

There are so many horrid stories of that time of me getting drunk and making a fool of myself. I was crying out for help inside, but just couldn't stop pushing the self-destruct button not seeing any way out. I was proving to everyone what some of them thought I was going to turn out like anyway, so in some ways it was easy to be like this. At least this way there was no expectation from me. If only they knew the heartache I was going through inside. How the mighty had fallen, I could hear some people saying in my head. I had gone from being on the school board, in the local drama group, being part of the community to a hopeless drunk at rock bottom seeing no way out of this living nightmare. Crying out to God, if he existed, to get me out of this living misery of life - to end it all once and for all, for this was certainly no life for me or my family.

Valerie Ashworth More

.

Some Of the Toughest Battles You Will Ever Face in Life Are Between You and The Old You.

CHAPTER TWO

Fine

My marriage ended, and to be honest it was a relief, but by this time I was dependent on alcohol. I couldn't function without it. I was emotionally, mentally, and physically done, every part of me was crying out for help. I couldn't even sign my name because I was shaking that much.

By this time, it was obvious I was dependant on alcohol. My friends persuaded me to go to the doctor. Between them, they convinced me to get help which I did. It was not very pleasant as I had been drinking for so long my body would go into shock if I didn't get professional help. I was admitted to hospital for detox. The first few days were horrendous, but slowly I came round and started to feel better in myself. This was the start of numerous hospital visits over the years, but in hindsight it was just putting a plaster on the problem. What I needed was someone to reach out to. It's nobody's fault in a lot of ways. The professionals just saw this drunk person coming in for detox, going home, and starting to drink again. What could they really do to help fix me, this broken empty excuse for a human being? Somehow, I managed to become organised for a while and it felt so good, what a difference waking up not needing a drink or crawling round the house looking in all my hiding places, desperate to find anything which would give me that hit. Saying these famous last words that I have said on numerous occasions over the years, 'Never Again'.

But who was I kidding? I never got to the real root of the problem and knowing I had to reach out to the only person who could ever help me, my Heavenly Father.

But a miracle did happen, I got myself together and I stopped drinking for two and a half years, and I felt good about myself, healthy and full of life. Seeing things from a sober outlook was brilliant. No hangovers. The guilt and shame were still there, but the difference in me was immense. I lost weight, started walking more and the boys saw a difference in me. My friends, especially Ann, got their friend back at last, well for a while anyway. When folk used to ask me how I was doing I would say 'FINE'. (A church friend has since told me she used to say the same, meaning 'For in Need of Encouragement'). It is a word that is used by almost everyone, but how are they really feeling? Does anyone bother to ask them? I know in the past I never used to either, but I make sure I do now. I always used to think it was just me that felt empty and broken inside. How very wrong I was.

When you are drinking in secret, you think you're the only one. Desperately searching through cupboards at four in the morning, hunting for drink, finding it hidden in the most bizarre places because you've forgotten where you've put it the night before, thinking that nobody knows what you're doing pretending to be sober, feeling so ashamed and alone, getting looks of distaste and condemnation because they didn't know any better. All folk could see was an annoying drunk, but it does not have to be like that. You do not have to feel FINE anymore, you can and be happy to be alive, full of Spirit (and not the Alcoholic kind), the brokenness gone. There is help there, other folk just like you are going through an addiction of some kind - Fear, Loneliness, Abandonment, Loss of Finances. Never lose hope and the belief that you do matter, and things can get better. My hope lay in God, but I just did not know it yet.

I am not going to be preaching to you about God in this book, it's a personal choice, it's about finding out what works for you. But he is the only thing that could really fix me.

After stopping drinking and feeling better in myself other thing started falling into place. My relationship with my two boys improved. It had been a tough time for them as well but getting their mum back sober was just what we all needed. Spending quality time with each other meant a lot, doing things that did not involve drinking, watching films, just having a decent conversation - something that we didn't really do when I was drinking. We went into the town, did things that we had not done together for so long, meeting up with friends who were so relieved to see me not drinking. I loved my garden, so it was nice spending time doing that, just puttering about doing normal everyday things. Life felt good, but I always had that nagging doubt that the urge for having a drink would come back. I prayed every day that it would not.

I was really enjoying being sober, felt a renewed sense of self-worth, it was great not to feel paranoid thinking everyone was speaking about me, or if they were it was hopefully positive things and to be honest, I did not really care because I felt so good in myself, and my boys were happy having their mum back. For the first time in a long while I could hold my head up high and that is something I never thought I would be able to do again. What a feeling, wakening up in the morning feeling fresh, putting the kettle on for a cup of tea rather than going on the hunt for a drink which I had hidden somewhere in the most obscure place the night before.

My youngest son was going to go into the Secondary School in Kirkwall, so I went and started doing a computer course on the mainland. I travelled back and fore every day on the local ferry which I loved. It felt like a fresh start. I also started going to Alcoholic Anonymous meeting once a week which was a real blessing to me as I finally found other folk to which I could relate. I was not the only one who was going through sobriety and their stories about when they were drinking really struck a chord in me. What a revelation it was hearing all the folks' stories on what made them start drinking and how they coped with their addiction. I also learned that you could have a normal life without drink, a better fulfilled life. I would recommend going to these meetings. I went faithfully for a few years and met some wonderful people who

came from all walks of life but who just happened to
have a drink problem. For two nights a week they
shared their story about how they started drinking and
how they managed to stop. It is somewhere you can go
and pour your heart out to like-minded people, because
we all had one thing in common that one jinx in our
armour - alcohol and the power it has over us and how
it really destroys life. It can strip you of everything,
your family, job, dignity, finances, self-respect. It holds
no prisoners. Like any addiction, you cannot beat it
alone, but there is such a lot of support out there if you
want it.

Around this time, I also got a strong sense of wanting
to join a Baptist church. I really felt God was crying out
to me. I remember sitting on the bus going into town
and thinking to myself where that came from. I mean I
believed in God, but this felt different. It really felt that
this was important and was going to be really life
changing which it was when I did eventually find one.
It was like coming home.

Wow - what a feeling.

I was so nervous the first time I attended the service,
but the folk were so kind and accepting of me, just full
of pure love and joy.

They really did treat me like their family, I told my testimony and what a sense of release, standing up the front of the Church. I was so nervous about talking in front of everybody, but I need not have worried, telling my story and looking out to all the understanding faces, some with tears running down their faces. I felt such a sense of peace and love. I was not scared anymore, and I didn't feel alone anymore either. The best feeling was that no one judged me. I finally felt accepted, something I have never forgotten to this day. Thank you, my wonderful Church family.

Oh, how my life had changed, from the drunken broken wife I had become to this confident happy soul that had finally felt accepted by folk that loved me for who I was. My mask was finally starting to come off, I felt so content. I was doing a counselling course at my local college, and I met two other members of my church that were doing the course. I really felt that God was bringing us all together and I now know it was no coincidence that they were doing the same course as me. It is amazing how he brings people together. What a wonderful time I had doing this course and I am so grateful that Mark and Val were there as well. I loved this time in my life everything was starting to fall into place and I was meeting new folk who I had a real connection with. I really felt that I would never drink again. I did not have to. I had my boys, my church family, my family, and friends. I had a good job; nothing could go wrong after all I had my Heavenly Father looking over me. In some ways I was so naïve, but that was me all over. When things were going well, I let my guard down, and that for me is when it is dangerous ground because what was lurking round the corner was something that was going to rock my very core.

Another thing that happened which was totally out of the blue was that I met my now husband, Andrew. Neither of us was looking for a relationship as we both had been through an unpleasant experience and so understandably, we were very wary of getting hurt again, but our friendship grew. We started going out together, just taking it very slowly at the beginning, baby steps. I used to think he is so nice in a way, too good to be true. Could someone be that perfect? I was starting to have feelings for him which felt scary as I really had made my mind up that I was not interested in another relationship. That chapter of my life was closed, I was quite content to be on my own for the rest of my days. That sounds very final but that is the way I felt. I just wanted the peace of being on my own. Little did I know that's how Andrew was feeling as well, so when he started having feelings for me it was scary for him too. Sometimes, though, these things are out of your control, and we went out on our first date. I was so nervous there was more rice over the table than I put in my mouth, but he seemed to like my quirkiness and the rest as they say is history. I just wish I had been honest with him at this point, but that is what I was like. I thought everything was fine and that is when things go so wrong for me.

All my family and friends and my two boys really liked him which was a relief, especially my boys. After what they had been through it was such a relief to me to see them getting on with Andrew. Unfortunately, and so stupidly I did not mention the fact I shouldn't drink. I suppose looking back I wanted him to think I was normal (whatever that is). I so wish I had told him right at the beginning. He is such a good man with values and morals that now I know that he would never have judged me, but for reasons I will never know, when he offered me that first drink instead of shouting at the top of my lungs 'NO I don't and shouldn't drink', I stupidly I said 'yes that would be lovely thank you.'

What a complete insane think to do, but I was a typical addict burying my head in the sand. Here I was, kidding myself that surely after two and a half years I would be fine. My body should have recovered in that time and was I really that bad before I stopped drinking. It is funny how you convince yourself that things were never that bad. All I had to do was say to someone that knew me that I had started drinking again and I know they would have been shocked and tried to make me see sense.

Do not Drink.

Alas, here I was with a glass of wine in my hand thinking this is not really going to hurt me. It is only wine after all. None of that hard stuff like spirits. What a silly fool I was, thinking I can stop at any time, but already enjoying that hit. Thinking about my next drink and hoping there was plenty in the house.

Of course, we had a great night with plenty of drinks flowing. I was having a smashing time. Every time Andrew went out of the room, I would sneakily pour more drink into my glass, so I was getting double the amount he was having. I was the life and soul, kidding Andrew I did not drink very often just a good session once a week. Do you see the pattern? Trying to kid him, but only kidding myself.

This is the point I should have been screaming out 'No I don't want this, I shouldn't be doing this', but instead I could not get enough drink down my neck. I was feeling so good I genuinely thought why I ever stopped drinking. I love this feeling, conveniently forgetting the hurt and pain I had caused everyone that cared about me before I stopped two and a half years ago.

In the morning when I woke up it took me a minute to realise what I had done, and then it all came back to me. Oh no, I thought, how could I have had that first drink? My poor boys, how could I look them in the face ever again?

Oh, the Guilt and Shame was back. Why Or why didn't I just tell Andrew before I took that first drink to my lips?

As I lay there, I got myself convinced that everything would be all right. I had not wakened up wanting a drink. I was still drunk, so of course the effects of the alcohol were still flowing through my veins. I felt rather good, no hangover, and when Andrew offered me a cup of tea and I accepted. I thought, I have cracked this drinking thing. I will not drink again for a while. I will control it rather than it is controlling me.

Phew I had got through this; I was going to be all right. Why did I think I had a drink problem? I could manage it, but why did I have that horrible feeling in the pit of my stomach that I was heading back downwards into the pits of hell?

Always be honest with yourself and others because in the end "The Truth Shall Set You Free," but hindsight is a wonderful thing. I have learned that regrets just eat you up inside and leaves you full of self-loathing, so if you can, learn to love yourself. You are a precious jewel and so loved by the one person who will never judge you.

Be Yourself No Matter What People Think, God Made You Unique and Has a Special Plan for You, When Hard Times Overwhelm You, Sadness Grips You or When You Feel Darkness Return Look Up Towards the Sun as It Holds the Promise That God Is with You That This Too Shall Pass.

CHAPTER THREE

Kidding Myself

So, I settled into a happy life with Andrew, a good solid relationship. I had a decent job, life seemed great. We both attended the local Baptist church. Previously I had gone to the Church of Scotland church where I grew up on Hoy and had always enjoyed the service but going to the Baptist church something came alive inside me. When they started singing the worship music, it was absolutely awesome. There are two Baptist Churches on the Orkney Mainland, one in Kirkwall and one in Stromness. On Westray, one of the outer North Islands, there is another.

Over the years they have become our Church family

and have seen me at my lowest point but have always been there to pull me back up from the pits of hell. There are some good people in this world, real Godly people, who take no credit or expect any thanks. Without them and their unfailing love I really do not know where I would be today.

As I said, life was good. As well as our Church friends we also had close friends outside the Church who were such support to us. I did a counselling course at the local college, which I loved. I really connected with the people who were also doing it. Even though I was drinking again, I was still able to function normally because I was managing to control it. Andrew was not a big drinker just a dram at the weekend, but I was starting to sneak more. Not every night at first, but I would use any excuse for us to have a drink, kidding myself that everything was fine and that I could still control it. What a crazy, all-consuming illness this is. It fools you, convincing you that everything is wonderful.

I would go off in my lunch hour and buy a half bottle of vodka for later just to give me that fix, but by now Andrew was starting to suspect something was not quite right. For a start, he could smell the drink on me, and he had been at sea for over twenty years working with fellow seafarers of which a few had drink problems. He could spot an alcoholic a mile away.

I believed I could outwit him and did for a while, until one night I drank a bottle of his wine that was in the fridge and filled the bottle with water. That was fine until he decided to have a glass himself and realised what I had done. I confessed and told him then I should not be drinking. The drink had got its horrible grip on me. He was very understanding and tried to make light of the situation by saying

"I've heard of water being turned into wine but never wine being turned into water."

Knowing Andrew, the way I do now, I know that was his way of dealing with the awfulness of it all. He uses humour to try and deal with difficult things. We can laugh about it now, but at the time I was mortified. I waited for the moment he would say to me that he could not do this anymore, but he never did. I was so surprised and grateful. Over the years, sometimes I wished he would give up on me to prevent the hell I put that man through. He deserves a sainthood.

Around this time, he got a job and went away to sea for a month. That is when the drinking got out of control. I was drinking every night and finally first thing in the morning too. How could this have happened again? I thought. Why oh why did I put myself in these situations, wakening up first thing and reaching for was a drink just so I could function? I could not even get out of bed without that much needed hit and as soon as it was in my system, I thought I ruled the world. Everything looked wonderful through drink fuelled eyes, so I would have a couple more just to make me feel human again (or so I thought). It was awful by this time. It could have been any time of the day, never mind first thing in the morning. Of course, I knew I had to go into work. Looking back if I had just phoned them up and said I needed time off to sort myself up I am sure they would have been understanding. Instead, I got the bus and went into work, half sozzled. and of course, I got the sack.

Oh, the devastation I felt inside. I had let everyone down again. How was I ever going to face anyone? I phoned my friend Ann, and she took me to her house and looked after me, getting me sober again. What a sorry state I was in. I was due to get Baptised at the Stromness Baptist church around this time, but I cancelled it. I could not face anyone. What a mess I was in. The hangovers were getting more severe when I was going through withdrawal. It took me days to get over the severe shaking, being sick and my heart beating so fast I thought it was going to explode. The worst thing was the paranoia, thinking everyone was talking about me and judging me.

Who could blame them, I thought, but most of my friends and family just felt heart sorry for me? I did not want their sympathy. Part of me was getting bitter, thinking why me. It did not seem fair that everyone else goes through life without any problems. Of course, self-pity is a trait that an addict has, a very selfish attitude, but that is the nature of the illness.

I managed to get sober and stay off the drink. Andrew was due to come home from sea. How was I going to face him? Surely, he would want nothing more to do with me after this, but amazingly he was so supportive. Unfortunately, this would not be the last time he would be facing this. We settled into being together again and I did not drink at all for a while. I really had loved my job and missed working, especially that feeling of pride I had enjoyed earning a wage and standing on my own two feet. The feelings of Guilt and Shame were back with a vengeance, but we moved on. We went back to the Church where they welcomed us with open arms. Andrew got a job at sea, month on month off. I was still based out in Hoy, but was spending more time with my friend Ann, who lived on the East Mainland. Eventually Andrew and I got a house and moved in together a fresh start which was exciting and meant I would have more chance of getting work in the mainland.

Things were good for a while. We got into a routine of Andrew being home for a month and then away for a month. I was working again, so life felt like it was back on track. Of course, when he was away the self-doubt would creep back again and that little voice in my head kept saying,

"Go on have a drink, you deserve it. One will not hurt you, anyway who is going to know"

So, I did. It felt so powerful, that voice in my head. I should have picked up the phone and spoken to someone, but it was too late. The drink was starting to take a grip again. Just the odd evening to start with. I was still attending Alcoholics Anonymous. They knew about my last slip, but I did not tell them I had started drinking again. Sitting at the meetings, pretending everything was okay, too proud to cry out for help, but then this voice would whisper in my head "why bother? I could handle it."

I was in control of the drink not the other way around. Who was I really kidding? How easily you forget the destruction and pain it causes when you start the downhill spiral of drinking again. Poor Andrew, just when things were going well for us, bang I threw it all away. This continued for a good while, stopping for a year then starting again. Sometimes when Andrew came back from his month on, I was ill. I had managed to stop before he came home, but the tremors, sweating and paranoia were all there. It took a good couple of days before I was fully recovered, pretending to him I had not drunk that much but he knew fine.

When he was away, I did not attend the Church very often, and never stayed connected with my family. My job was coming to an end as I couldn't be relied upon, and I never really told Andrew how bad things were. When I was not drinking, we had really good times. We would go on trips together and everything felt so perfect. Why did I keep going back to this horrible torment that was drink? I lost good jobs, pushing all the folk that I was close to away, because I did not think I deserved to be happy. Always a part of me thought I had better throw it away before it got taken from me. It is only now, twelve years later, that I realise I am good enough for Andrew. I could not count the number of times Ann would come in and find me laying on the floor after another bout of binge drinking, not knowing the worry I was causing everyone that cared for me. What a terrible shame and a shock for her, thinking I was dead. Of course, I was fine just sleeping off the effects of the alcohol, oblivious to what was going on. I am so sorry my friend.

Eventually Andrew got a job locally on one of the Ferries. We had bought our own home by this time in Kirkwall, giving a sense of security I had never felt before. We had so much to live for. People would tell us what a special couple we were. I certainly felt really loved, but there was still this sense of not being good enough for him - always a nagging doubt in my head.

I went for up to a year without drinking and boy did it feel good. My family were back in my life, I was working, and we were attending the Baptist Church. I finally got Baptised and that was so wonderful. What a blessing I felt. I was a new creation, reborn, but as happy as I was, my good friend self-doubt came back, and it was 'here we go again'. I started drinking, and each time it was getting worse. A part of my soul was slowly dying, and I felt I was dragging Andrew down as well. When I was drinking, he started dreading coming home from work, not knowing what he was going to find. He started noticing a pattern in my behaviour. I could go for up to a year without drinking, he would let his guard down and I would slowly start to change my moods. That was when he knew it would not be long before I started drinking. I could kid myself I was okay, but that is all it was – kidding.

I pushed him to the limit many a time, but it shows the true value of the man that he is, that he never gave up on me. He always loved me. Who would have blamed him if he had? My family and friends were at their wits end with me. How many times would I keep on pushing the self-destruct button for him to finally have enough? Thankfully and miraculously, he stood by me when others really could not take any more of my yo-yo drinking. I cannot say I blamed them It is a sad sight to see someone you care for destroying themselves in front of your eyes, in and out of hospitals, detoxing or lying on the couch after having another fit. A pitiful sight. Sometimes Andrew was more of my carer than my partner. I was feeling sorry for myself, not thinking what he was going through. My eldest son was a good ally for him, someone he could speak to when he was at the end of his tether with worry, not knowing what this outcome would be and when the drinking would ever end. His biggest worry was me dying because how could a body take such a hammering that I was putting mine through?

Somehow, I survived the abuse I was doing to myself (I now know it was God's protection that kept me alive)

Life was like that for years full of ups and downs, being referred to Alcohol Counsellors who do a fantastic job and help so many people, but for me it never really helped. It never got to the root of the problem. I still had an empty void inside. That FINE word always came back to haunt me, and when I did stop drinking and sobered up the Guilt and Shame came back with a vengeance. My job gone again, my self-respect, feeling so sorry for Andrew having to go through this again, back to being broken Val with the mask back on. So, we plodded on happy in between bouts of drinking, thinking this time I had cracked it and had beaten the demon drink. Never again I would say to myself. We went to Church, went through the motions but not really reaching out to God. Just kidding myself that I was okay.

How wrong I was, things were going to get a whole lot worse.

Our Lives Are Storybooks That We Write for Ourselves, Wonderfully Illustrated by the People We Meet

CHAPTER FOUR

The Enemy Within

I was a typical addict in that when things were going well, I stopped doing the things that helped me stay sober. I did not go to Church as much as I should have done, stopped attending AA, didn't stay connected with my close church friends who I usually met with once a week at least. It really was a feast or a famine with me, all, or nothing. I have learned since this is a life commitment. You cannot just pick up the pieces when you decide, when you have gone through another drinking session. If you are committed to God, then it is a twenty-hour day commitment, not once a month when you're coming off the drink, praying for forgiveness and pleading with him to get me through the night. When the tremors and shaking comes when you do not have that drink, it really is a nightmare that you can't wake up from. Your heart thumps so much you think it is going to explode and then when you do fall asleep you waken up with a start, feeling that you're going to die. So why do we do it time and time again to ourselves? Why do we think this time is going to be so different? You know when you take that first drink what the outcome is going to be, but you convince yourself that this time you are in control. You can manage it. You conveniently forget the horrors that you have left behind and what is going to be in front of you.

when I first started drinking all those years ago and it was getting a grip of me, it would take a peedie while for the alcohol to really affect me. Now after just one drink I was a jabbering drunken wreck, sweating and already planning from where to get my next drink. I always made sure I had enough for the morning because it didn't bear thinking about what I would be like if I didn't have any in the house. Once or twice, I did not have any and that was the worst feeling, pacing up and down, hoping I wasn't going to get withdrawal before I got my fix, clock watching for the shop to open so I could go and get my first drink, hoping no one saw me buying drink at that time of the morning. In the end, I did not really care who saw me. I just wanted to get that hit inside me rushing through my body. I could not look at myself in the mirror, because all I could see was this pathetic drunk staring back at me, an ugly red bloated face ravaged by the drink. How could I have got so low? The lowest point was when I was going through Andrew's wallet, looking for enough money to get me a drink. He tried everything to stop me buying it, thinking he was helping me. There was always plenty to eat in the house, but that is not what I was interested in when I was drinking.

I would drink all through the morning, feeling better since I had my drink inside me, but sit ting in front of the television not really watching it, just feeling like a complete waste of space. Andrew would come home in his lunch hour. Sometimes and I would try to act sober in front of him, but he knew I was drinking so by the time he came home in the evening I was a jabbering wreck, full of self-pity, promising him I would never drink again. Another endless trip to the doctors to get tablets for detoxing was like a vicious circle.

I managed to stop for a few months got my life in order, got a part time job, got back on track again, and so things got back to normality. We were happy. I was so thankful not to be drinking. By this time Andrew did not really drink anymore, firstly to support me and secondly, he was sick of it. It used to be a sociable thing for him to do, but it had turned into something he despised. We sometimes went out for a meal when I was off the stuff and that was nice, because when I was not drinking, I didn't crave it. I never thought about it, that is why the doctors were baffled with me. I never struggled when I was sober, just when I had that first drink things went downhill.

So, in 2013 I got the job of my dreams I had not had a drink for a long time. I felt good in myself. We were starting to feel that we would like to get a house in the country, get out of the town, but we could not really afford it as I was only working part time. Even though Andrew was working full time, the house prices were a bit out of our reach, so when I got this job, it finally felt that things were changing for the better for us. Finally, we could see the light at the end of the tunnel. We both had good jobs and we decided to take the plunge and buy a house outside Kirkwall. The house of our dreams came up for sale on an island off the mainland called Shapinsay, a twenty-minute journey by boat. It was perfect for us. We loved the house instantly and the island was so beautiful we decided to go ahead and put an offer in to buy our dream home. The sale went through and so here we were with our lovely new house on a great island, and the view was amazing overlooking Veantro Bay. Everything that we had ever hoped for had come true.

Oh, how perfect life felt at that moment, for the first in a very long time I could see the worry gone from Andrew and replaced by happiness and contentment.

What a year it turned out to be. We got married and I passed my driving test. How could anything get more perfect. I let my defences down for the first time in a long time. I thought that things were going to be okay, but life has a habit of getting in the way. Bad things happen, things that you don't expect, I loved my job, felt really fulfilled and I hadn't felt like that in a really long time. Surely this was it. No more drinking or suffering. This was the happiest I felt since my boys were born. I had it all. A great husband, a brilliant job, my boys were happy, we had the home of our dreams, I felt so proud of myself, and at long last Andrew wasn't worrying himself sick over me.

We went away to London on holiday to see my brother, thinking that things were all fine. I had a wonderful time away, but when we got back things were not very nice at work. Folk were not being genuinely nice. We were under a lot of pressure, and I started drinking again, and this time with bells on. This was the ultimate one, the one that just about destroyed us. I lost my job. This was my rock bottom (or so I thought). We could not see a way out of this one.

I remember Andrew sitting on the chair in the living room putting his hands up to God and saying:

"That's it, there's nothing more we can do."

He was right. We were wrung out emotionally, physically, and most of all spiritually. Here we were back to square one, him having to face folk at work and in public knowing that we were getting spoken about. (Orkney is a small place and most folk know you). Having to go away to work for two weeks at a time, worried sick about his wife at home, wondering if he was going to get that dreaded phone call. What a crying shame. The pressure that poor man was under. How he did not have an emotional breakdown with all the stress and worry I will never know, but since then we have learned that it was the Lord that was keeping him strong.

I just could not stop drinking this time. If I am honest, part of me didn't want to. I wanted to give up and drink myself to death. I felt so ashamed, back to rock bottom again. I was a nothing - an insignificant piece of worthless rubbish. That is how I felt about myself and I imagined that's what other folk thought about as me as well. How selfish this disease is, (because it is a disease), but all you can think of is yourself. Andrew at work and me laying on the sofa drinking myself to death, but that is the nature of the beast.

You do not see at the time how it drags all the ones closest to you down. You just think of yourself, poor me syndrome. I could not see a way out this time, thought it would be best if I just left Andrew. For even though I was drunk a lot of the time, even selfish, drunken me knew this was wrong. It was no way for anyone to live. He had to be better off without me, I thought, but he did not want me to go. He still wanted the marriage to work. He could see the real Val he had fallen in love with inside this broken drunk wifey,

One day Lynne a Christian friend of ours came round for a visit, and she said she had heard of a place called Betel, it was a place, run by volunteers, where broken Christians could go to try to rebuild their lives. When she first suggested this, I thought, no way. I do not need to go to a place like that. I was married and had a lovely home. I would be all right, I could stop drinking when I wanted, (wow how the enemy was fooling me), but thankfully God had other plans for me.

After about a week of endless drinking, a dear church friend of ours, Marion, came over to visit me from the Stromness Baptist Church. She and Lynne were praying for me and Margaret a lovely lady who was like a mum to me sat with me, making sure I was all right. They were worrying themselves sick about me. What a sight I must have looked, all bloated and stinking of stale alcohol, not showered for days. I must have stank, but they hugged me and told me how much they loved me and most of all how much God loved me. In the end even I knew that something had to change. I decided enough was enough. I was beat, the enemy had won again. It was time to get help.

The folk of Shapinsay were so kind to me before I went away to Betel. We had not been on the island long, but I will never forget how they treated me with such love, special people.

So, after my first drink of the morning to steady the shakes and tremors I went round to Lynne's and told her I was ready to go to Betel. I just could not do this anymore. I spoke to a lady on the phone who was so nice to me. I kept thinking why you are being so kind, if only you knew me you would soon realise what a bad person I was. I did not deserve kindness or pity. If I were a decent human being, I wouldn't keep on drinking and hitting rock bottom and hurting the people that loved me the most. She kept telling me how worthwhile I was, and I was going to get better.

Oh, what lovely words. Was it possible that this broken excuse for a human being could get better? As she said, the ball was in my corner. I had to want to get help. My time away in Betel was not going to be a walk in the park by any means, but I got this strong sense that this was going to be a turning point. It was arranged I was to go in the next couple of weeks. They do not usually take married couples, but they must have taken pity on me as they agreed I could go. I would highly recommend it, if you feel you are at rock bottom, and have nowhere else to turn, and have a faith in God.

Andrew came off duty and a couple of days later we headed to Hexham in Northumberland, a very nerve wrecking and scary journey that was going to change our lives. I had to drink all the way down because my body would have gone into shock if I did not. What a state to be in! The car must have stank like a brewery, but Andrew never complained. Even though we knew this was the best thing for me, it was still extremely hard as there was a possibility, we might not see each other for up to a year. When he dropped me off that day, it was awful. It felt like my heart was being ripped out. I remember begging him not to leave me there, but he was strong enough to know that for the sake of our marriage and for our future together we had to do this.

It was one of the worst things to ever happen to me but also one of the best. I did not realise how hard, challenging, brilliant, soul searching these next few weeks were going to be.

"Ships Do not Sink Because Of the Water around Them. Ships Sink Because Of the Water That Gets in Them. Do not Let What's Happening Around You Get inside and Weigh You Down.

CHAPTER FIVE

BETEL 2015 Amazing Grace

I was at Betel for five weeks. The first night was tough. I was crying, missing Andrew, and going through cold turkey. By the evening I was feeling thoroughly miserable. My whole body was starting to go through withdrawal, desperately needing a drink. Since I was feeling so awful the ladies decided to do "Candles" with me, where they each take a turn staying up with me through the night to make sure I was all right,

I was so ill I thought I was going to die, but they stayed by my side like my guardian angels protecting me. At some point during the night, I needed to go to the toilet. One of the girls had to help me up the stairs. I could not walk, crawling up the stairs with no strength in me and shaking all over. When we came back down to the living room, she put her hands on my shoulder and prayed out to God to help me get through this. She prayed over for me a good hour. After a while I felt a calmness coming over me like honey filtering through my veins. I fell into a peaceful dreamless sleep. When the morning came, and I woke up and was so surprised that I had slept. More amazingly, I had survived the night. To this day I honestly believe that God put his arms of protection around me, keeping the enemy from attacking me. I really believe in the power of prayer to do miracles in people's lives.

I still felt dreadful the next day from the alcohol withdrawal, but not as bad as I thought or should have been. God was already starting to work inside me. I missed Andrew terribly, but unbeknown to me he had started on his own journey with God and what a story that is. To this day I really feel that God needed to get us apart so he could work on both of us.

Every morning we went to the Chapel before we went to work. I did not want to go that first morning, but it was expected of us. There was a Pastor there that lives in the grounds with his wife and family, The Chapel was amazing, what a feeling of Peace and Tranquillity there was. The worship music reminded me of our local Baptist Church back home in Orkney. One of my favourite songs is Amazing Grace, My Chains are Gone, I have been set free. When everyone sang that I was in tears (there was a lot of shed tears in that five weeks at Betel). I was missing home, but at the same time God was sending me a message, telling me that everything was going to be okay.

The first weekend was tough. I was so homesick, crying all the time, but as time went on, I got settled into a routine. You get allocated a job every day. Betel is a charity, and the men and women go out to work to take in money to help the upkeep of staying there. My favourite job was working in people's gardens.

I was also starting to feel stronger in myself. My body was slowly starting to repair itself from the damage I had done to it with months of endless drinking. My favourite time was on a Friday night and Sunday Morning when we went to Chapel. I really felt at one with God through Prayer and Worship. What an amazing journey I was starting to go on. There were things from my past I had to let go, people that I had to forgive, before I could really move on with my life. You do not realise what a burden you are carrying around.

One Friday night I went up to the front for Prayer and

the Pastor was talking about Forgiveness. He was saying, what right did we have not to forgive, when Jesus forgave us on the cross for our sins. Why shouldn't we forgive anyone that has wronged us? I knew then that I wanted to let all my burdens of forgiveness go and forgive. So, I did. I was on my knees at the Cross begging for forgiveness and forgiving all who wronged me. Suddenly I felt this powerful force inside me. I started shaking and something left my body. I have never felt anything so powerful. It felt scary, but so good at the same time.

The demon that had been battling with me all these years was gone; the heavy burden was lifted from my shoulders. Over the next few days, I felt a change in me, I was growing inside spiritually, something I never thought could happen to me.

In life some of us go through so much pain and emotional trauma, usually at the hands of someone else. Sometimes it feels overwhelming, and you cannot see any way out. Please believe me when I say there is a way out. You do not deserve to be treated this way, always remember how precious and worthwhile you are. You do not have to be living this way. Nobody deserves to be in chains, so it is time to break the bondage that is keeping you prisoner and break free.

There is help out there, people do care, I care, and God cares.

Sometimes when I am looking out my living room window overlooking Veantro Bay I go into my own little world and think back on my life, and it feels like it was happening to a completely different person. I suppose in a lot of ways it was from the person sitting here now, but I honestly believe that things happen for a reason. Do not get me wrong. I would not wish to go through the nightmare again, but if just one person reads this book, and it helps them then it will have all been worth it.

I WILL KEEP SAYING THIS, not to preach or be bossy (well okay just a little bit) but because I care. NEVER GIVE UP. Life is worth living and things will get better. BELIEVE IN YOURSELF.

One thing that kept me going while I was away at Betel was the cards and letters that family, close friends including church family sent me, and the phone calls from Marion and Tina. Without hearing their comforting voices, I would have felt really lost. It was touching to know that they were thinking and praying for me and knowing that people do care for me, that I am worth it.

While I was there another thing, I loved hearing were folks' Testimonies - what had happened in their past that had made them hit rock bottom and then turn their lives around. It really hit home and here I was crying again, but it also made me feel humble and honoured that they felt they wanted to bare their soul to other people. That is no easy task I can tell you, but a very brave thing to do. It gives you hope to know that through tragedy there can be a happy ending, maybe not the ending that we wanted but at least we were free from our demons and God was starting to be in control.

One evening before bed I was chatting to one of the ladies and I said I felt very selfish because I had so much to be grateful for. Her answer surprised me. She said STOP RIGHT THERE. Do not ever feel selfish or grateful. It is what you, anyone, deserves.

Even me?

Why not me?

We do not come into this life asking for heartbreak or troubled times. It is a basic human need to feel safe and secure and our God given right to have a good, happy life, free from Guilt and Shame and from addiction. So, you see, even though I had gone through the whole forgiveness thing the old Val was still lurking around with her self-doubt, not feeling good enough. There was obviously a lot of work to be done yet, but as usual I thought I had it all sussed out.

HOW WRONG I WAS.

You see there is no quick fix. It takes Time, Patience, Love, Hope, Faith, but in the end, it is worth it for Peace and a mending of the Spirit, Soul, and Mind as well as the Heart.

My time at Betel was coming to an end. One day while out working in the gardens I asked God when he thought it would be time for me to go home. One word came into my head "Patience" Everyone at Betel had in their way Set Me Free from my Demons (Thank you my Angels), but I was starting to feel that I did not belong there. That is not anyone's fault. It is just circumstance. I had a husband, a home, and a family to go back to. How Blessed was I and I certainly will never take that for granted again.

One night while I was sleeping, God spoke to me in my dreams and told me it was time to go home. So, my time there had come to an end. I will always be eternally grateful for my time at Betel, for my Darling Angels who helped me through so much. The folk I met will stay with me forever, but it was time for this particular journey to end. Andrew came down from Orkney to pick me up and take me home. We were ready for the next Chapter of our lives.

He had been on his own journey with God, which came as a bit of a shock to us both, for so long it had always been about me and my addiction,(how selfish that sounds now)trying to get me better, that we didn't realise that God wanted to come into his life and what a revelation it was, a full week of transforming unique experiences, while he was at work as well, thankfully there was fellow Christians by his side ,thank you everyone who was there for him especially Marion a true blessing from God, so much happened but it changed Andrew forever and to this day he has a strong Faith which enriches both our lives every day. We have both changed for the better, we certainly felt a lot more at peace.

But unfortunately, the Nightmare was not over just yet, not for a while anyway.

Focus on Your Strengths Not You're Weaknesses
Focus on Your Character Not You're Reputation
Focus on Your Blessings Not You're Misfortunes

CHAPTER SIX

Our Walk of Faith

When I left Hexham to go home, I felt like a new person, a new creation you could say, and I truly was. The enormity of what had happened to me in the previous five weeks, the transformation that I felt inside, still hadn't hit me. Andrew also looked so alive, happy, and full of the Holy Spirit. It felt and was amazing, we had so much to talk about it was so exciting. Anyway, he suggested that instead of going straight back to Orkney we go via the West Coast of Scotland, through Fort William. What a brilliant idea I thought, so that's what we did.

We stayed in a hotel that night with the famous mountain Ben Nevis in the background. It felt so good to be together again after being apart for five weeks. In the morning we went down for breakfast and Andrew said the immortal words

"Do you know how we've always said we would like to climb Ben Nevis someday"

I said, "Yes we have right enough."

(I had a funny feeling what was going to come next). He then said Well, we're not that far from it. Let's take the plunge and climb it this morning. My initial first reaction was Gulp. No, we can't. We're not fit enough, but the new Val, the one that didn't have the self-doubt said, "Yes Let's Go for It."

To this day I think our family and friends think we were bonkers climbing up and down the mountain, but that morning it felt like we could do anything we put our minds on, and of course we had God there to help us. So, we got packed up, went downstairs to pay the bill and the receptionist said,

"What are you doing for the rest of this beautiful summer's day?"

In unison we said, "We're going to climb up Ben Nevis."

Well, her face was a picture. Here were these two slightly unfit Orcadians, standing in front of her smiling away like a pair of schoolkids ready for our big adventure. She must have had some laugh when we left. I mean normally you train for weeks to get your body into top peak condition, but no not us. I will never forget the look on her face as we got ready to leave. Mind you, if she had seen us a few hours later that would have been some story to tell her friends. What a sight we must have looked.

But onwards and upwards quite literally. We set off on our epic journey full of so much enthusiasm. It was around nine o'clock in the morning, a lovely July day. It usually takes around five to eight hours to get up to the top and back down again, so we thought we would be back down by teatime. No bother to us. We were used to walking, we could handle it. No bother to us outdoor types from Orkney.

So off we set, looking the business with all the gear on, walking boots, rucksacks, camera, drinks of water, sweets. Oh boy we looked the part, feeling really excited about the whole experience and of course we had God to help us get to the top. The first half went well, a walk full of contrasts, quite flat in some bits but very stony and rocky in others. As we headed upwards, of course, there were always people passing us old and young alike. It was quite enjoyable, such a bonny day and stupidly I thought this is going to be fine. We will do this no bother. God must have had a chuckle at this point.

As we were getting closer to the top, we both started to struggle. Folk who had overtaken us on the way up were on their way back down. Now that was soul destroying. I was starting to think this is not going to be so easy after all. When one of us struggled, the other one would urge them on, and we also prayed over each other which gave us the strength to continue. Near the top I was really finding it difficult, I really felt that I couldn't go on. It was too hard, every part of my body was in agony, I was crying so I said to Andrew,

I CAN'T GO ANY FURTHER, YOU CONTINUE WITHOUT ME,

NO, HE SAID, YOU'VE COME THIS FAR, YOU CAN DO IT, AND I DID,

*So, Here's What I've Learned. Don't Give Up,
Don't Be Impatient; Be Entwined as One with The
Lord. Be Brave, Courageous and Never Lose
Hope.*

CHAPTER SEVEN

Nothing is Impossible

What a feeling when we got to the top of Ben Nevis. The weather wasn't great, windy, and snowy. By this time, we didn't have the energy to take any photos and there was the horrible creeping feeling that we had to walk all the way back down, but we had each other, supporting one another. It was something Andrew was used to doing with me over the years. On the way back down, the view was spectacular; we really felt God's presence with us, giving us strength to keep going.

We finally got back down the mountain, and what a feeling of achievement it was. Oh, if that girl from behind the reception desk could see us now. We were really starting to feel the burn in our legs and feet, but to think we had climbed up that mountain, and came back down again. Words can't describe it. I passionately believe we were meant to do that walk-up Ben Nevis. It really was A Walk of Faith.

At times I really did not think we would make it to the finish, but with determination, supporting one another and knowing that God was beside us encouraging us, We Did It.

That is why I genuinely believe nothing is impossible. If you want something bad enough, you can do it; with Gods help (and a little bit of sweat and tears). Never give up your hopes and dreams. There is no such a word as CAN'T. You can do anything your Heart Desires, so if it's Beating an Addiction, having Faith in yourself, a fresh beginning, starting a new job or even climbing a mountain, go for it. At first if you feel nervous or scared, keep going. Be proud of yourself and if you stumble or fall get back up, dust yourself off and start again. The sense of achievement and self-worth you will feel is worth every bit of frustration, tears, fears, and strength you thought you never had. You are a beautiful, worthy, individual person created by God. One of a kind who can do anything you want to do. Go for it. You deserve it.

Keep Going, Difficult Roads Often Leads to Beautiful Destinations.

CHAPTER EIGHT

I am Truly Blessed

So, we had done it, climbed a mountain. Our Walk of Faith.

It was now time to go home to Orkney, back to our Sanctuary, Veantro. I felt so excited, but a little bit nervous going back to Shapinsay to face everyone again. After all they didn't know what a transformation I had gone through. They hadn't met the new Val yet. I hoped they liked her. Coming home was the best feeling in the world. I felt so very Blessed.

I need not have worried. The welcome home I got from folk was overwhelming. I must admit it was a bit daunting, going out again in public to the local shop, the hub of the island, but everyone was so kind. Thank you all to the folk of Shapinsay. You really are all amazing, a great big, blessed hug to you all.

Shapinsay really feels like home to us now and our beautiful home Veantro is just the icing on the cake. So now time to get back to living a normal day to day life, no longer in the bubble of Betel. It felt so good to be in my own home with all my familiar surroundings. Life goes on which is good. I need structure so it's good to have a routine every day, especially when Andrew is away for two weeks. It's nice when he's home for us to do something different, unexpected, out of the ordinary which we do. Life felt good. Surely now this was our fresh start? We could at long last look forward to a bright future.

When Things Go Wrong as They Sometimes Will.

When The Road You're Trudging Seems All Uphill.

When The Funds Are Low and The Debts Are High

And You Want to Smile but You Have to Sigh.

When Care Is Pressing You Down a Bit,

Rest If You Must, But Don't You Quit,

Success Is Failure Turned Inside Out,

The Silver Tint of The Clouds of Doubt,

And You Never Can Tell How Close You Are,

It May Be Near, When It Seems So Far,

So, Stick to The Fight When You're Hardest Hit,

It's When Things Seems Worst That You Must Not Quit.

CHAPTER NINE

The Long Road Home

This is where the story should end, the happily ever after that we all want, but there is more to come. Life felt good, Andrew had just recently been reunited with his birth father, so we went down to Bury in Manchester to see his dad John and his step mum Barbara. It was a very emotional time. They were so supportive of us both. It was only the second time they had met me. The first time I was bubbly Val with a decent job on the local ferry back home in Orkney, this time I had just been away at Betel getting help for battling alcohol. What would they think of me? But they embraced me and told me they loved me. What an amazing couple.

I felt so happy for Andrew having found his dad after nearly forty years. It turned out to be a lovely holiday. We went to Yorkshire to see more family Lee, Tina and their four brilliant children, Olivia, Cameron, Alisha, Katelyn, a truly inspirational family.

Since I was going to be home more, we decided to get some pets. We got our first little kitten from our neighbours. We called her Smog, a little ball of grey fluff, and she was awesome.

Of course, life isn't a fairy-tale and Andrew still had to go to work to pay the bills. It was tough with just one wage coming in, but we were happy.

We attended the Baptist Church every Sunday, kept fellowship up with our Church family, just kept busy, following the Lord. I got a job locally for a few months which was a big help, but slowly slowly catch a monkey the doubts started creeping back in. I started thinking I wasn't good enough. How are we going to manage? It's just the enemy trying to play mind games with you. It's like your mind is a battlefield with all the spiritual warfare going on the whole time. Sometimes I felt like I had no control of my emotions, happy one minute, and low the next. That mask was starting to come out again. I felt so disappointed in myself, what a failure.

I suppose in hindsight I still had the Guilt and Shame about losing my job and not working. I had forgiven at Betel, which was all gone, but I don't really think I had dealt with the drinking, if I am honest. Not that I was wanting a drink. I hadn't thought about it for months and of course I was cured in my mind. Life was better without it.

Another thing I hadn't let go off was always wanting to please everyone, never saying NO, taking things on and rushing around really busy. I suppose that was my way of not having to think about what was going on inside my head. I wanted Andrew to be so proud of me which he always was, but I felt I could strive to be better. Oh, how I wish I had spoken more openly about how I was feeling inside, but things were going good in our life. It was just the self-doubt in my head that was the problem. As usual I didn't stay connected with my Church family as regularly as I should. That old habit of when things are going well, I think I'm fine (remember that word) and I can manage on my own. Who was I trying to fool?

But life goes on. I felt content and happy most of the time. I was busy every day. For me, if I'm busy helping other folk then I'm "ACCEPTED" and don't have to face up to the real me, fighting all the negativity away.

We got our darling puppy Ben. He certainly filled the time in. I liked the fact that there was something that was relying on me, and of course all that unconditional love. What a Blessed life I had, so why did that self-doubt keep rearing its ugly head?

*Your Greatest Test Is When You Are Able to Bless
Someone Else When You Are Going Through
Your Own Storm.*

CHAPTER TEN

Fill Me with Grace

Orkney is a lovely place to live; I have many happy memories growing up on the Island of Hoy. An idyllic childhood playing on the beach in Brimms, (it wasn't so great after that but that's another story). We didn't have much money, but as a peedie lass I was oblivious to all that. My sisters Brenda, Ella and Margaret and I were very close and were always there for each other, especially Brenda who was the oldest, but looking back I'm glad I have three sisters.

I remember the Summers were warm, but there was always a breeze, I suppose that's because we're surrounded by water. We never went away on holiday, but to me living in Brimms and playing all day on the beach was the best fun I could ever have.

I still see the folk I grew up with and there is definitely a sense of caring about one another. The other thing about living on a small island is that everyone knows you, what you are doing and how you are living your life, but I count that as a blessing, a real sense of Community Spirit. There is always someone you can go to and have a chat with, pour your heart out to. If you ever feel the need to speak to someone that you can trust, go to them, don't keep things bottled up inside. It will eat away at you. Knowing that someone is there for you that doesn't judge you, knows your strengths and weakness is important. That's one thing we don't do - judge others. It's a destructive emotion. Always try to be happy for one another no matter what your circumstances. If you're feeling happy or sad, are in a bad place emotionally, spiritually, financially always bless someone who you might think is better off than you, because the value of wealth is how you treat other people no matter how rich or poor, they are.

When I lost my job, I had to really pray to God to give me Grace and to be thankful for what I had. Surprisingly with all the drinking and damage that I had put my body through I was very healthy.

Sometimes when I was alone in the evenings, I would think to myself if only I hadn't done that or had done that differently, but that's when the enemy gets into your thoughts and really goes to town. That Guilt and Shame rears its ugly head once again. So always try and look at the Positive things in your life. Thank God I have a brilliant husband and wonderful family and friends; I was going to need all the love and support from them very soon.

Valerie Ashworth More

The Only Person You Should Try to Be Better Than, Is the Person You Were Yesterday.

CHAPTER ELEVEN

Thank You for Your Love

So after about a year since coming home from Betel I was starting to feel like I needed a full-time job. Where this came from I can only guess, but I suspect it was the Enemy playing mind games. (If I'm honest with myself I was feeling guilty about not working so he had a stronghold to work on). Looking back, I wish I had waited. PATIENCE is a word that I'm starting to understand, but back then I wanted things yesterday.

Not once did Andrew make me feel I should get a job. I knew if I wanted to stay home full time that was fine with him, but I wasn't listening to that. All I could see, and think was that I need to work. I would feel more self-confident and independent if I were working. I really did have a different way of thinking from most people, rushing around not listening to the folk I should have been paying heed to.

I applied for a job, without discussing it with Andrew, which in hindsight I should have, but I wanted to "surprise him." I got the job, I was finally in employment again, my Pride was back. (They do say that Pride comes before a fall). In the twelve years that we have been together it's only now that I can accept that Andrews wage is also my wage. I never could get my head round the thought that his money was my money, even though he told me often enough. It must have been really frustrating for him when I acted like this, especially when I wasn't working, and I called it his money. But that's all changed now, looking back it makes sense why you're like that. When your mind is programmed to think in a certain way, it takes years, and someone with a lot of Patience and love for you to change your mind-set.

When I told Andrew that I had got a job he looked genuinely happy for me, if not a little shocked. He asked if I thought I was ready to go back to work full time and typically my first reaction was of course I am. Why wouldn't I be? After being home for a few months and loving it, he could see a real difference in me. How blessed I felt being home in the place I loved surrounded by our animals, (by now we had a dog, two cats, nine hens and four ducks).

He saw in me a newfound confidence and a peace that he hadn't seen before. Veantro is a magical place, so quiet and tranquil, it gets deep down into your soul, your very being, and makes you feel cleansed and glad to be alive. Understandably he was a little bit worried about me going back out to work again, but I was genuinely ready for it, and I loved my job. It was so perfect, there was not one single part of it I didn't like. What a feeling of pure contentment and joy it was. I was busy, but that's what I had been craving for. I didn't have time to think about me. Every single of aspect of our life was Perfect, my home, my marriage, my job, my family, and friends, and then out of the blue GUESS WHAT.

"I STARTED DRINKING AGAIN,"

That voice in my head saying go on one won't hurt you.

I tried fighting it myself, never told Andrew how I was feeling. I wasn't speaking or praying to my Heavenly Father as much as I should have been, and not making an effort meeting for fellowship with my Church family, always too busy doing something else. There are other Christians on the island, but I just didn't get round meeting up with them or confide in our local vicar.

So, the Guilt and Shame was back with a vengeance. The family I was working for were so nice and supportive to me and I am so sorry for drinking and breaking their trust. How could I do such a shameful thing? I ended up in hospital this time but discharged myself. I didn't want help, just wanted the pain to go away. I went to stay with family. Friends of ours on the island, Allison, Margaret, and Jenny looked after the animals as Andrew was away at work on the boat.

So, I kept on drinking, could not face up to the shame this time, and found it hard to even contemplate sobering up. As far as I was concerned my life was over. That sounds very over dramatic, but that's how I genuinely felt. So disillusioned, I came back to Shapinsay and continued drinking. When Andrew came home on leave, he took me back into hospital where I detoxed for five days. I was so ill it was awful, but the nurses were so good to me. They don't get enough credit for the work they do, certainly at my local hospital "the Balfour." The doctor who examined me said I was lucky to have survived this last drinking binge, at this point I can honestly say I didn't feel very lucky.

So here we were going again it was all about ME ME ME.

I came home to finish my detox with Andrew looking after me, (poor fella) What a state I was in, but at least I was sober (not for long). While Andrew was home, I was okay, but still felt horrid, like a piece of dirt on someone's shoe. I wouldn't let Andrew tell any of my family or friends this time. I was just too ashamed; I was back down in the gutter.

But he did tell our dear friend Pat from the Baptist church and she came to see me in the hospital. She is such a lovely Godly woman, what a blessing she is, but alas it was time for Andrew to go back to work. I was fine for a couple of days, but I just felt so ashamed. I couldn't sleep, I felt really scared, so very paranoid thinking everyone was talking about me as if I'm that important, but do you see the pattern? It's all about poor me.

So inevitably I started drinking, the hard stuff this time, neat vodka. When I had run out and had no way of getting it, I would go knocking at the neighbour's door, begging for drink. What an affront. I just kept drinking for two weeks with friends trying to ration me so I wouldn't drink too much, but I was fly - a typical addict. I always seemed to get hold of drink. To everyone I am so terribly sorry.

So, Andrew came home on leave and slowly I came off

the drink. Of course, it was tough for a few days, but I slowly started to come round. Eventually glad not to be drinking. I would like to take this opportunity to thank everybody who helped and cared for me when I was going through this. You know who you are. You were so kind and supportive to me, kept me in your Prayers, A big heartfelt thank you.

It took me a long time to even go out the front door. The guilt, shame and self-loathing were back in abundance. The enemy had ground me down again, only this time he had nearly won the battle. Thankfully not quite, but if I had carried on drinking who knows what the outcome would have been?

So here I was back at rock bottom once again. I had no job and had let everyone down again. I just could not see a way to get back up again. I just wanted to hide away in my own self-pity. But there was one thing I hadn't counted on, my Church Family. The amount of support we got from the Kirkwall and Stromness Churches was unreal. Such kind thoughtful messages, phone calls, letters, e-mails. It was truly an amazing feeling at my lowest, but still there were folk still loving and caring for me, Marion, Linda-Ann, Pat, Barbara. We all met up. There were lovely messages from Irene. The Baptist churches entwined in their love for us.

They were amazing people. Thank you for your steadfast love and never giving up on me. I Love you all from the bottom of my heart.

We found out about RTF (Restoring the Foundations) from our dear friend Lynne. A couple ran it down in Stirling (Scotland). Andrew and I discussed it and thought it would be a good idea, to speak to them on the phone. It was arranged we would go down in July. They also asked Andrew if he wanted to do it and he said yes, as its good for couples to do the Ministry Counselling together.

Valerie Ashworth More

You Are Going to Be Everything God Created You to Be, Walk Free with Him, Don't Follow the Wide Path Follow the Narrow Path to Happiness.

CHAPTER TWELVE

Healing the Soul

RTF (Restoring the Foundations) was founded by Chester and Betsy Kylstra in America but is now also run in this Country. It is for folk that need healing and who believe in God and that Jesus died on the Cross for our sins.

The need for Healing is realising you have a problem in your life, pain from what others have done to you, pain from addictions and pain from what you've done to yourself.

I'm not going to go into what RTF involves, that's for you to decide for yourself. All the information is on the Internet or get in touch with us and we can direct you to the people who run it in Scotland, Stuart, and Helen Hammond.

So off we set on the 1^{st of} July on the Ferry from Shapinsay to the Orkney Mainland, and then on to Saint Margaret's Hope (another part of the Orkney Mainland to travel on the ferry Pentland Ferries to take us to Gill's Bay travelling to the Scottish Mainland.

Then we drove down to Stirling to start the next chapter of our lives. It felt so good to be doing this together. We were both a bit apprehensive, but also very excited about doing this week's ministry, knowing this would be a big turning point in our lives.

I honestly didn't know how it would work. Nothing else had. What was going to be so different about this? We arrived in beautiful Stirling, a place that holds such good memories for me and some bittersweet ones.

The first time I had visited was with my two boys who absolutely loved William Wallace the Scottish hero, so the Wallace Monument and Stirling Castle was a special memory for me.

So here we were driving up to Stuart and Helen's house, my heart beating so fast. Andrew was quiet which meant he was deep in thought. I really felt God's presence, and it was like he was physically sitting in the back seat of the car.

The moment arrived as the Sat Nav says, "you have reached your destination." Never had I heard such a truer thing said even though it was from a computerised lady's voice. How surreal that was, God really has a sense of humour.

We parked the car and the front door opened and this lovely lady was standing there welcoming us. The first thing I noticed about Helen was her bright shining eyes, so pure and white, full of love and hope. I trusted her right away. We gave each other a hug and that's the moment I knew that this was going to be a life changing experience for both of us. Then Stuart greeted us, a man that you instantly knew was full of the Holy Spirit.

What a place, it was their home, but also a haven - somewhere for you to open your heart and speak about your most innermost secrets and hurts, things you've never spoken about before. I always told Andrew some things, but it just hurt too much to tell him everything. Partly because he was too close to me.

I had things buried inside me that I never wanted to talk about. They were locked up inside my soul and I didn't want it to be unlocked. I had thrown away the key a long time ago because it hurt too much.

But slowly as the week went on, I started to mend with God at the helm and Stuart and Helen as the vessel. I realised that God had that key that was locked inside me all I had to do was open up to him and he would mend my broken soul.

We had separate Ministry times, me in the morning and Andrew in the afternoon. I started seeing a change in him. Things that he thought he had dealt with came to the surface. You really do bare your soul, but it's what you need to do. An amazing experience.

But why was I so surprised when God was in control? All I can say is different things work for everyone. I'm not telling you to go to RTF. I just know it worked for us. It changed my mind-set, made me realise I am worthy, I am loved, I do deserve happiness but mostly I AM A CHILD OF GOD, his beautiful Princess of the Orkney Islands.

Leaving at the end of the week we both knew that our lives had changed for the better. It was a bit scary as well for us as we had been in this awesome bubble for six out of this world's days, a cocoon of such pure love and kindness, and dare I say holiness and pureness.

To think I had used drink to fill a void, when all along the answer was staring me in the face, "Surrender yourself to the Lord and leave your Fears at the Cross."

Thank you, Stuart, and Helen. They take no credit, but they have such a passion and caring for others, a genuine Godly couple who we had the privilege of meeting and doing our Ministry with. Thank God for people like them, but mostly thank you to our Heavenly Father. For the first in a long time, I can face the future without fear, feeling a failure, emptiness and instead I am a new creation.

Someone who can face the world with a new confidence, knowing that anything is possible as long you believe in yourself and know that you are so loved.

Valerie Ashworth More

Your Heart is the Size of an Ocean, Go Find Yourself in its Hidden Depths. You Are More Powerful, Imaginative, and stronger than you can ever Imagine.

CHAPTER THIRTEEN

I've Finally Come Home

I hope you have enjoyed reading this book, if enjoyed is the right word. I pray that you have, and for someone it might be just what you needed to get through another day. For me writing it seems so surreal. Never in a million years did I think my life would have turned out like this, but then it's not so bad, I have a lot to be so thankful for.

I can look at myself in the mirror now and not flinch at the person looking back at me. I'm surprised that the pain has gone from my eyes; the wear and tear of all the years of drinking has lifted. My eyes look like they are shiny and clear. No makeup in the world can be this good, even though I am 53 years old I feel so much younger.

I am a different person now, a new creation. Life has changed me, but the mask has gone. What you see now is the real Val, a bit more reserved, quieter, but as Andrew says that's maybe not a bad thing. I'm at peace with myself and reflect a lot. I no longer think "IF ONLY," it's such a waste of energy. Life moulds you into what you are, be proud of who you are.

God has given me a new beginning. The Scripture passage, "I will renew your Strength and you Shall Mount up on Wings like Eagles" is one I have always loved, but now I know how true and wonderful it really is.

We are all totally unique, wonderfully made. Be what you want to be, it's your life. Don't let anyone tell you what to do or put you in a corner. If you're in a bad place right now just remember it can and will get better. Don't be alone, know that you can make that change. TAKE THAT FIRST STEP TO FREEDOM.

Life without drinking just gets better and better. It's a beautiful place to be, you see things clearer and brighter. It really is a joy to be living. I always thought that to get on in life I had to be liked by everyone. I now know that it's an impossible goal to achieve, too much pressure to put on yourself. Not everyone is going to like you, but hey that's okay, there's plenty that will.

I'm happy now being on my own with Andrew and having my family and friends around me. By starting to like ME, I'm comfortable in my own skin. So, start liking YOU. Give yourself a break, don't be so hard on yourself, start off by getting to know yourself and eventually by liking yourself. You are on the road to being set free and finding your own identity.

I love my life now and believe me I never thought I could. It's a peace that comes within, deep in your soul. When Andrew goes away to work for two weeks, I still miss him, but I have learned to enjoy my own company and not feel guilty about being home full time. Not away working but looking after our animals.

In the past I always put pressure on myself thinking that I had to work to bring a wage in to please Andrew, but now it would be nice to bring a wage home just to help financially and get job satisfaction. Looking back, I was like a pressure cooker waiting to go off, exploding. Now when he comes home on leave it to a calm, sober, happy wife, so I am truly blessed. I love my solitary life, but I also enjoy being with the lovely folk living on this idyllic island called Shapinsay.

When we were at RTF, God showed Andrew two lines from the book Women, Thou Art Loosed, by T, D JAKES, NEW KINGS JAMES VERSION. It really summed up our lives for the last twelve years,

"Now That God Has Brought You through the Crisis and Raised You up to Maturity, You Are Ready to Enter the Fullness of this Destiny for you,"

So here we are now, entering a new Season of our lives, I really feel that God is starting to use my past for other people's futures. And that's exactly what I want to do. What an honour and privilege that would be. I have finally found my identity and come home. It's taken over Forty years, but I'm fulfilled with God's peace, and now it's so good not to feel Guilt and Shame anymore.

I've come face to face with all my demons and won the war against the enemy. And so can you. Reach out to our Heavenly Father, he's waiting for you and enjoy the magnificent journey that's in front of you.

It's now over five years since I had a drink and it's been an awesome time full of more highs than lows. As I walk our dog Ben on this beautiful cold snowy January day, I feel so glad to be alive. I have such a lot to be thankful for and I know without Gods will and blessing it could all have been such a different outcome. Looking over the water to the Outer North Isles where Andrew takes the ferry back and forth to

Kirkwall, carrying passengers, it seems like a lifetime ago since I worked on them. I never thought I would get over not working on them, but I am so much happier now, more contented and at peace with myself. I have learned that you don't need a job with a huge salary. Find what makes you happy and it nourishes your soul. That's worth more than any pay check.

The simple things in life are what mean the most to me now, being home with Andrew and our animals, spending time with family and friends. Finally, I have battled my demons no more guilt or thinking I don't deserve this.

Life is a challenge, nobody said it was going to be easy, but it doesn't have to be filled with drama. You don't have to feel shameful or that you don't deserve to be happy. It's your right as a beautiful creation of God to be happy. Don't let someone else's failures bring you down.

Never Let Go off Hope. One Day You Will See That Everything Is Finally Come Together. What You Have Always Wished for Has Finally Come to be.

You Will Look Back at What Has Passed, And You Will Ask Yourself, "How did I Get through All of That"

God Bless You as You Enter the Game of Life,
Striving for your Destiny.

Printed in Great Britain
by Amazon